GOD, I've gotta talk to you!

prayers for Children
written by Anne Jennings and Walter Wangerin Jr.
Illustrated by Jim Roberts

ARCH® Books

COPYRIGHT © 1974 BY CONCORDIA PUBLISHING HOUSE, ST. LOUIS, MISSOURI

MANUFACTURED IN THE UNITED STATES OF AMERICA

ISBN 0-570-06086-9

In the Morning

Dear God, I thank You for this day
    That's only just begun,
The pearly dew upon the grass,
    The newly risen sun.
Be with me in the busy hours
    And lay Your hand in mine.
Please let the path I walk be bright,
    With loving deeds ashine.
Teach me to know You and to pray.
Dear God, I thank You for this day.

A. J.

About The Seasons

Sometimes I run with my arms wide apart,
Green grass in my feet and the speed
    in my heart.
Sometimes I leap into brown autumn leaves;
I crunch them and punch them;
    I breathe them and sneeze.
Sometimes I give the cold snow a good place
To land on in winter: my hands and my face.
And sometimes in spring, when the earth
    is unpeeling,
I thank You, my Lord, for Your world
    and my feeling.

W. W.

About Forgiveness

F ind me, Lord; I'm small as a pin.
O h, I get tiny when I sin!
R each down behind the garbage cans,
G o back and forth with both Your hands —
I 'm small, I'm dirty, but I'm here,
V ery unhappy, full of fear,
E xpecting soon to disappear . . .

M y Jesus, find me, then I will be
E verywhere, carried there by Thee!

W. W.

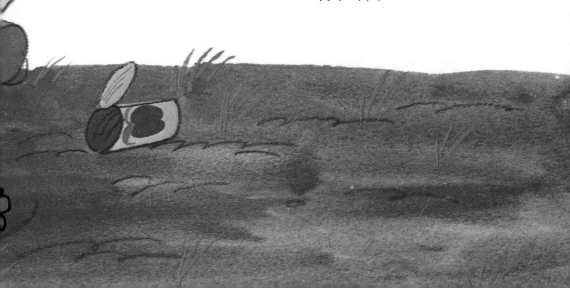

About Being Forgiven

A strange thing, Jesus, makes me cry—
When someone *else* is hurt and I,
I know *I* hurt that other guy,
　　His hurt becomes my own.
But Peter hurt You, didn't he?
And You forgave him, set him free.
Then, Jesus, please remember me;
　　Don't leave me all alone.
Please help my friend forgive my sin
And make us then what we have been—
　　Two friends who love like one.

W. W.

About Forgiving Others

Lord, once when You were hurting
    through and through—
Cuts in Your feet, Your side, Your hands,
    Your head—
You looked on those who did this thing to You
And cried for them, and this is what You said:
"Forgive them for they know not what they do."
Oh, Jesus, sometimes people cut me too.
Teach me to look on them with peace, with love,
Forgiving them as You forgive above.

W. W.

When I'm Happy

Times come, dear Jesus, when my smile
Stretches like rubber for half a mile;
And then it breaks and then I laugh
So hard that it aches for a day and a half.
I laugh at anything, I guess—
At leaves, at lunch, at words like Yes.
Thanks, Lord, for so much happiness.

W. W.

About Flowers

I thank You for the flowerbeds
Where lilies, roses grow,
Bright hyacinths and sweet peas too,
Some pansies in a row.

The lovely blossoms that You send,
   Those named and others too,
Are like some happy little smiles
   For me, dear God, from You.

A. J.

About My Family

F rom my father, a sturdy love,
A nd from my mother one like prayer;
M y brothers and my sisters shove
I nto my life because they care.
L ord, let them know I love them, too.
Y our love's the key; we learn from You.

W. W.

When I'm Lonely

Times come, dear Jesus, when I find
Nobody here to play with me;
Like crows they chase away from me,
And I'm the last one left behind.
Dear Jesus, You were once alone;
You know my feelings to the bone.
Then be my Friend, make me Your own,
Love me, love me; be here, be kind,
And always keep me in Your mind.

W. W.

When I'm Afraid

I couldn't count, dear Lord, the things
　　That sometimes frighten me:
An open window five floors up,
　　The deep holes in the sea,
The dogs who flash their teeth by day,
　　The angels of the night,
And death, and life, and things to come,
　　Things loud like dynamite.
But none of these can separate
　　Me, Jesus, from Your love,
For You are with me here below
　　While You're with God above.

W. W.

At Meals

Our health is given by this food;
Our food, dear Lord, comes by Thy grace.
Our thanks we offer in return
At every meal, in every place.

W. W.

*   *   *

Dear God, I thank You for this food
  As well as I am able.
Please bless it, Father, to our use,
  And be our Guest at table.

A. J.

About Sick People

H ear my prayer, Lord, for the ill:
E ncourage them while they lie still
A nd give their restless spirits rest.
L ead them through the painful night,
T hrough fevers, needles, dreams, and fright;
H eal their bodies, their spirits bless.

W. W.

About Friends

I thank You, Father, for my friends,
    Who are so close to me.
We laugh and play; at school we work
    So very busily.

I thank You for my special Friend,
    Who lays His hand in mine
And looks at me with loving eyes,
    Like candleflames ashine.

I thank You for His gracious love,
Which never has an end.
I thank You, Father, for Your Son,
My Brother and my Friend.

A. J.

About School

S uddenly summer is no longer here;
C hrist, come with me to the next thing this year:
H ands raised to answer questions wrong or right,
O ld friends and new, and homework for the nigh
O ur teacher, paper, pens—it all smells new.
L ord, in my learning now, let me see You.

W. W.

At Night

The night is dark and silent now;
Make darkness good and silence rest.
Lord, let my sleep tonight endow
Me with Thy peace and blessedness;
And if the morning comes to me,
Grant me laughter, life, and Thee.

W. W.

DEAR PARENTS:

There are times when children's hearts are so full that they spontaneously spill over into prayers. There are times when children take great comfort in repeating the words of the old familiar prayers—"Now I Lay Me Down to Sleep," "Tender Jesus, Meek and Mild," and, of course, "Our Father." But there are also times when the words won't come and when a special prayer, a prayer just for children in a specific situation, works best. Then it feels good to read a prayer about being lonely or afraid or in the painful position of having hurt someone else. Or to hear someone else read it for you.

Help the child understand that there are many ways to pray: in groups, alone, in shouts, in whispers, in songs, in tears, in thoughts. And assure the child that we have God's promise He will always hear our prayers.

THE EDITOR